AF375278

THE PAPER SUN

4-Year-Old Jenny Dawn Learns That the Best Gifts Come From the Heart

SUZY COWELL

DEDICATION

The Paper Sun is dedicated to Suzy's children, grandchildren, great-grandchildren, and those who will follow. It is also dedicated to teachers—those who make so many personal sacrifices to help all students reach their highest potential, no matter the starting point of their abilities.

Jenny Dawn, a girl of four,

is a girl who all adore.

Big blue eyes, cheeks of rose,

sweet right down to her toes.

Christmas time: she thinks of this... *What can I do to bring some bliss?*

(How silly she is to think that she would be capable of bringing glee!)

Our Jenny Dawn, darling lass of four, remembers the bedridden woman next door.

If I were old, what would I like? Oh, not a doll or bright shiny trike.

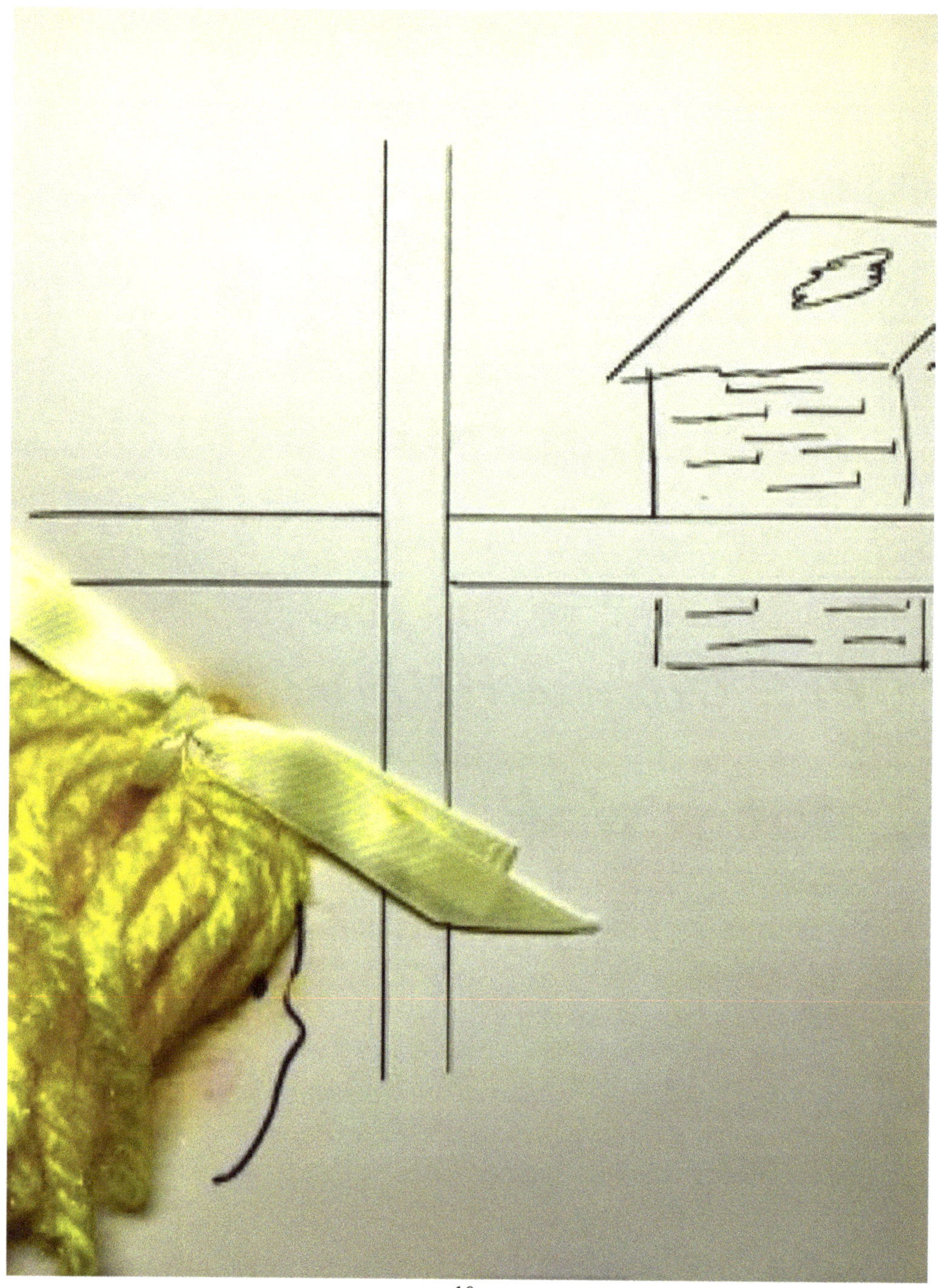

She has no window; it would make me pout,

to miss the view day in and day out.

I've an idea that I can use to
chase away Mrs. Lindsey's blues!

I've cut a circle; my gift is done.
I hope she

likes my round paper sun.

I need some ribbon to wrap my present.

I hope it makes her Christmas pleasant.

A few days later, Mrs. Jones chanced to stop in and give Mrs. Lindsey a glance.

"There she was," she told friends and others,

"Dead as could be, still under the covers.

Poor old thing, she's better off,
not able to walk, and such a
cough!

There's one thing, though, I can't
explain...the smile on her face:
no sign of pain.

And a yellow circle so raggedly cut was taped on the bedpost in her tiny hut.

Oh well, strange things are to be expected from one so old and so neglected."

Jenny Dawn's gift was tossed out and burned.

But to each of us a lesson learned.

You see, it matters not how small the gift <u>OR THE GIVER</u> is at all!

ACKNOWLEDGMENTS

The Paper Sun was written and illustrated by Suzy Cowell and kept in the family for almost a half-century before it was published. Suzy's children assembled the poem from pictures of the original, hand-made artwork to demonstrate Suzy's amazing talent for creating inspiring life lessons from simple things found around one's home. As a woman of great faith, Suzy has honored her Lord, her family, and her community for over eighty years with the countless stories she created. These and many other teaching tools she developed will continue to bless teachers and students of multiple generations in her community for years to come.

ABOUT THE AUTHOR

Suzy Cowell lives in Tennessee and is the mother of four, grandmother of eight, and great-grandmother of twelve. The story of Jenny Dawn is one of many stories Suzy wrote to share with her family at Christmas in order to encourage generosity, thankfulness, and gratitude among her family and friends.

Suzy received her B.S. degree in Elementary Education and has her Master's and Educational Specialist degrees from Tennessee Technological University.

As a professional special education teacher for over forty years, she taught children and adults with special needs such as visual and auditory impairments. She also taught Adult Basic Education and spent thirty years teaching home-bound students who had various temporary and long-term illnesses.

Her children published this poem to honor her and bless future generations of readers by awakening the spirit of Jenny Dawn that is within each of us.